GEEZERHOOD

What to expect from life now that you're as old as dirt

by Wayne Allred

Illustrated by David Mecham

◆ A WILLOW TREE BOOK ◆

Published by:
Willow Tree Books
Box 516
Kamas, Utah
84036

willow @ allwest.net
www.willowtreebooks.com

ISBN 1-885027-06-0

Cover Design & Layout by David Mecham
Printed in the United States of America

II

Certificate
of
Official
Geezerhood

Given this day _____

to _____

for Living Past the Age of
Bodily Function and Well Into the
Age of Mental Collapse.

Bestowed by the Aged and Arthritic

W.A.

Contents

Introduction

As I was walking past a group of retired orchardists and farmers who daily guard the entrance to some of our stores here in town, I overheard a group of teenagers saying disparaging things about them. My ears really perked up when I heard one of the girls repeat the infamous words that are haunting millions of baby boomers across America at this very moment; Those immortal words of Linda Rhonstadt or Richard Nixon, or somebody, that have become one of the defining themes of our generation, and, which at some time in your life even you have probably been guilty of saying, or at least thinking, namely: "I hope I die before I get old." I don't know about the rest of you children of the 40's, 50's or 60's, but, as mentioned above, these words make me wince.

I remember how I used to fear growing old. No more. I don't even mind losing what's left of my mind. I am one with nature. I understand my role in the cosmos. Besides, I'm pretty much composted.

I'm sure that those young people who were concerned about our local geezers, probably lay awake at night worrying about becoming senile. And it's possible that many of you who have rolled over the hill of maturity, moseyed up the summit of seasoned sagacity, and who are about to go caroming off the cliff of fossility are wringing your hands as we speak.

If for whatever reason you have found yourself pre-occupied with becoming a crotchety old geezer, we suggest you read on.

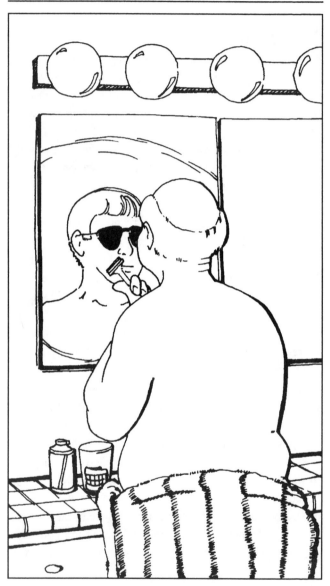

1

Looking at Your Future as a Fossil

If you are like most people, it probably doesn't seem all that long ago since you were a teeny bopper looking at people who were the age that you are now and seeing nothing but a drooping bag of varicose veins, flab, wrinkles, and dentures. You probably said to yourself in disgust, "I hope I'm dead before I get that old."

Here you are. You are that old. Sometimes you feel a little like a drooping bag of varicose veins, flab, wrinkles, and dentures. Yet, you are not completely dead. The amazing thing is, now that you are getting up there in years, you realize that being older might not really be all that bad. In fact, you look back and think, "I'm not so sure I would want to be 20 again...unless I got to take my brains and experience with me."

Oh sure; you could easily do without the loss of memory, back ache, bleeding gums, fatigue, loss of memory, sore joints, bad heart, loss of memory, extra weight, hemorrhoids, chronic indigestion, loss of memory, arthritis and loss of memory. And the loss of memory can be tough too, since, you don't comprehend what's trendy, and have trouble learning and remembering new stuff. Plus, the financial part can be the pits because your kids are breaking you, the government is milking you, and no one wants you working for them even if you felt like working, which you don't because you're so old, decrepit and beat up. So you're broke.

Aside from these minor inconveniences, if you're starting to 'geeze' you have probably concluded that, life probably could be a whole lot worse. At least the parts that you can remember. . . compared to the alternative. And at this point you're just not ready to end it all just to find out what's really on the other side.

The biggest problem you face is your fear of the unknown in your future, what there is left of it at least. You are losing the capacity, energy and disposition to deal with irritating (new) and uncertain things. When you had reflexes, strength, energy, and a memory, contemplating the unknown future wasn't so scary. You felt that whatever came up you could deal with. Now, with all of the experience you have gained, you know better. You need an expert to advise you of what's in your future. Because frankly, as you look at people older than you, you think things like, "I hope I'm dead before I get that old."

The purpose of this book is to provide enough information that we can successfully eliminate your fear of a geriatric future. Yes, after reading this book, you will probably be certain that you want to be dead before you get that old. This book could answer all of your questions about growing older...at least the ones that you can remember, and it will most likely deal with a few that you probably aren't even interested in.

We are able to provide these trivial insights because besides being older than many forms of dirt ourselves, we have observed many people, some even older than us, for years. Moreover, for our age and in spite of the fact that we have arthritis, bad backs, hemorrhoids, arthritis, gout, gingivitis, arthritis, chronic indigestion, nutritional fatigue, arthritis, lower back pain, hair-loss, osteoporosis, Alzheimer's and arthritis, we still have remarkable memories, a quality we find exceptional for our age.

We believe that because of these terrific powers of memory, we are just the persons to write this book and grease your slide into senility.

By the way, did we mention that we have arthritis? ◆

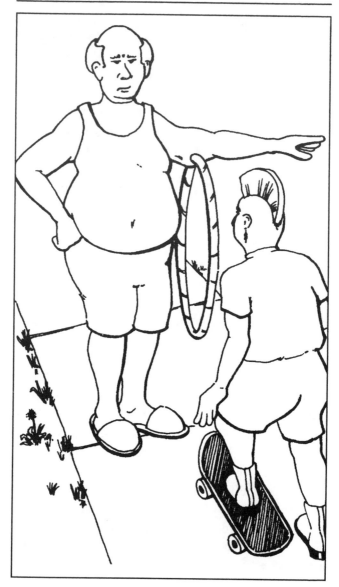

Are You A Geezer?

As they start to get older, many otherwise normal people wonder whether youngsters have begun to perceive them as cratchety old geezers. Since there are no widely recognized standards and no government tests for geezerhood that we are aware of, we offer these symptoms which might give you some indication.

You might be a geezer if:

Whenever you wax nostalgic, even if you can't remember where you put your high school yearbook, you can still see pictures of all of your old friends by looking in the obituaries.

When you're proud of your 1968 Buick Riviera because when you went to get the mail this morning you side-swiped another car, backed into the corner of the tattoo parlor, ran over two dogs, scared the milk out of a cow, missed the east bridge by a hundred yards or so, and the car looks every bit as good as when you left this morning. (Incidentally, the only accident you noticed at the time was the side swipe, the other stuff you found out from reading the police report.)

New wrinkles are covering your body at roughly the same rate that the rain forest is being depleted...and you think the two are somehow connected.

When the younger generation has such ugly hair cuts (and you're convinced that they do it just to annoy you) and so to get even, you intentionally grow your nose hairs out and coif them into a bouffant.

When you one-up the neighbor kid by having an old Hoola Hoop punched through the skin sagging from your arms...and it hardly hurt.

When you are more familiar with, and would rather listen to, the sound of the doctors cracking open your chest cavity than your grand children's music.

Medications that you once took in small doses for purely recreational purposes, you now take in restaurant quantities to try and stimulate your organs to keep functioning.

When you have calluses on your butt from taking baths in tubs that have slip-proof safety sand paper in the bottom.

When the oldies stations are all playing songs too new for you to recognize

When you have the teeth of a back-woods Mississippi hockey player from all the times you slipped and whacked your face on the safety railing on the side of your tub.

When your wife has more hair on her face than you do on your head.

When the neighbor's dog barks in the night, waking you up, you roll your wheel chair over to their yard and strangle it with your oxygen hose.

When you suffered through Desert Storm, The Viet Nam War, The Korean War, W.W.II, The Great Depression, 15 years of MASH reruns, The Punic Wars, The Hundred Years War, and The British Invasion and so you know that you're entitled to your Social Security, Medicare, Medicaid, and the New Deal. If the slacking younger generation doesn't want to pay for it...shoot 'em.

When the bags under your eyes are larger than your shoes.

When you can convince people that your varicose veins are really a full-body tattoo of an over-lay of a series of Picassos superimposed over a slick of the Amazon Delta.

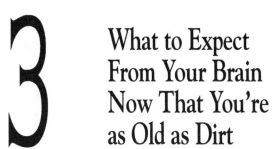

3 What to Expect From Your Brain Now That You're as Old as Dirt

In order to put your mind at ease, I would like to provide information to help you better understand the decline in your mental capacity as you grow older and allow you a modicum of peace of mind.

First, though, we need to clarify a few things. "Senility" is a highly unpopular term. It has been used in the past to describe many different mental conditions which are very different in many respects, and which modern medical professionals have now individually re-classified. Some examples are: "old timers disease," "redemptia," "consumption," "stupidity," and "senility."

Using broad generalizations and simply calling everyone who has symptoms of an embarrassing degree of memory loss "senile" is highly unfair, especially to those who are obviously suffering from the advanced stages of one of these other specific diseases. We ignorant laymen are simply over simplifying their condition calling everything "senility," or sometimes "stupidity."

So in order to be sensitive to those suffering from these specific diseases, and to do our part to use correct language so as not to offend anyone, and to keep you, our over-aged reader from becoming even more confused, we're simply going to refer to each of these diseases as "senility."

Now, with that out of the way, in order to give you greater peace of mind, I would like to describe some of the changes that are going on inside that decaying mind of yours. (I'd also like to get my grand-kids to eat zucchini and turn mosquitoes into $100 bills, but since I can't do either of those, I will settle for offering my version of "your slipping mind.")

More ways to tell if you are a Geezer

When, after 7 years of intimate friendship and great conversation you finally noticed that the guys you have been sitting next to downtown on the bench are really bronze gargoyles.

First, if you could look inside your mind right now, you would probably observe that it is a gooey, disgusting blob. And since none of us who are normal have the stomach for probing around stuff like that, let's just move on and consider mechanically what's going on in there.

Imagine that your mind is a very complicated CD player. It is filled with all kinds of high-tech doohickeys, most of which we can assume have some practical use. Now imagine that CD player caught an average of 2 or 3 colds per year for 30 or 40 years, and every time it caught a cold, big gobs of mucous ran down inside those delicate, little parts. After decades and decades of having this mucous pile up like this you can imagine what the inside of that CD player is going to look like. It's so disgusting that your grand children can't even look at it. I think I may have to go throw up. It's amazing that a mature mind functions as well as it does.

When your doctor can't tell where your hemorrhoids end and your varicose veins begin.

When people considerably younger than you are dropping like flies from age-related degenerative diseases.

It's at this point that the little CD player wants to get out some of your old Beatles, Frank Sinatra, Moody Blues, and Steely Dan records and listen to them, which, of course it can't, because it's a CD player and all you have are record albums. Not only that, but it's a CD player that is so complicated to operate that you can't even figure out how to set the clock on it...no, wait...that's the VCR. Anyway, music is played on CD players now days. Never mind that, YOU just happen to still have 500 "classic" record albums which you would love to hear, but which you can't because you can't even buy a record player any more. And so, after years of frustration, you just give up and use your records as symbolic Frisbees. In the psychological profession, we call this condition "Turn-Table Retentive."

You can easily see that after having had this kind of experience, your brain has no choice but to go into overload and start acting "senile." Knowing that eventually we all will have this experience, (yes, even you teenagers) let me offer a few suggestions: First, if you happen to have a really nice turn-table that is compatible with modern high quality stereo equipment, you should let us know.

Second, you should start today doing all kinds of exercises to get the old brain in shape, things like thinking in place, aerobic meditation, cardiovascular contemplation. Most of us psychologists do this by sitting in our favorite chair and dreaming of high-cholesterol "brain foods" that we love, but which we can no longer eat because they give us heartburn... foods like rhubarb pie ala mode, banana splits and sweet n' sour liver casserole.

And finally, think of ways to enjoy your brain while you still have it. After all, you might just as well concentrate on reading and viewing things that you like, since Gilligan's Island reruns will provide you with just as much retrievable information later on as your Calculus class, once your brain shuts down and you become senile. ◆

4 What's in Store for Your Body Now that You are Chronologically Disadvantaged

Now let us attempt to explain to you what is going on below the afore mentioned brain.

Remember when you would come busting out of work or school looking for a pick up game of basketball or flag football to use some of your pent up energy? Can you remember when you would go nuts if you had to sit out of the game for one minute as you chomped at the bit to get back in? Me neither.

Do you remember how, when you started getting a little bit older and more out of shape, you took up jogging or cycling sporadically. And how, in order to satisfy your need to remain physically active, but not hurt yourself, you took up softball or tennis? Me neither.

19

How about when you got to the point that, as those nagging pains from all your accumulated sports injuries mounted and you just didn't feel like killing yourself any more, you switched to golfing and walking to try to delay the onslaught of degenerative diseases? Can't remember that either? You are definitely an old geezer.

Now you look forward to your physical condition declining to the point that you will get your muscle tone and aerobic fitness from such activities as scratching behind the dog's ears, gargling and working your way through a good bowel movement. Your conditioning exercises consist of breathing in place, sitting in place, and aerobic eatersizing.

I'm sure that by now you are perfectly aware of the pathetic state of your body. What you may not understand clearly is why, when you used to feel so good all of the time, that this has happened to you. We will attempt to explain:

Everyone gets a vacation once in a while. School teachers, construction workers, executives, even the Pope goes skiing when he needs a break. But your body parts have never ever had even one vacation. This is not such a big deal when they are young and naive and obnoxious, but as they get older, say around age 40, some of those organs begin to look around and realize that they are being taken for granted, that they are not being treated fairly...And they begin to resent it big time.

At first, as they become mildly irritated they react by threatening to do such things as file a grievance with the department of business regulation demanding that you quit eating fat and get 7 hours of sleep a night. Later as they get more worked up, they begin to do small, yet slightly meaner things to you, like give you heart burn and make you run to the bathroom every half hour, and they begin to steal little things from the work place like pencils, wrenches, car keys and glasses.

When it becomes apparent that this is not getting them any closer to their goal of a vacation, (And after all, we can't blame you either because who wants to grant their kidneys or Gaul bladder a vacation?) they begin to grow more and more angry and militant. While, at this point they generally stop short of murder, their ways of getting back at you are getting progressively more uncomfortable. At this stage you might get seriously debilitating kidney stones, severe back pain, impotence, delusions of grandeur, Mad Cow Disease or migraine headaches.

Finally, after a few years of systematically and progressively cranking up the pressure -- without so much as a 3-day weekend, one by one your valuable body parts begin to go on strike, beginning with those who are most angry (normally the player reps) and then they completely shut down.

You should know that many things can be

done to slow this process down. You can take vitamins, eat a healthy diet, and get adequate sleep. We do, however, want to caution you about exercise. While in the short run you may think that exercise is helping, in the long run it will backfire. Your body parts are already overworked and exercise can make certain parts, like your heart, lungs, and major muscle groups, work even harder...with no hope of a vacation.

We recommend, to keep your body as happy as possible, that you begin by having a frank discussion with all of your body parts, in private of course. (This assumes that at this point your brain is still on your side and not beginning to join the protest movement too. If you've lost your brain, you are way past help.

Even more ways to tell if you are a Geezer

Although you're not sure whether it's due to dementia or your actual age, in any case, you can clearly remember the Napoleonic Wars, The Renaissance, Genghis Kahn, Linden Johnson, and where you were when Julius Caesar crossed the Rubicon, but you have a miserable time coming up with your children's names on short notice.

What you might say:

#1 First, to buy yourself some time, you might try the friendly, non-confrontational approach. Explain to them that you're in a tight spot and can't spare any one right this minute. Be sure and promise them that when you get past the busy time that you will let them have their vacation, one tissue mass at a time, beginning with the reproductive organs.

#2 If it's already too late to try and humor them and your body parts have reached the militant stage, you must take courageous and decisive action. Have your lawyer send them a letter outlining the penalties they will incur if they don't live up to their part of the agreement. This may buy you some time, but, since this is really just a bluff because they will eventually remember that they never signed any agreement, they will eventually see through it and you will then need to resort to something like:

When you are annoyed that everyone around you mumbles so badly that you have to ask them 2 or 3 times to repeat themselves before they speak loudly and clearly enough that you can understand what they said.

#3 Throwing a tantrum. Include loud threats of removal and transplants. You can make this even more dramatic by taking some totally useless body parts like your appendix, toupee or wisdom teeth and ceremoniously feeding them to the dog or your pet alligator to show that you mean business.

In the long run, nothing will work. At some point it will become apparent that the best thing to do is to begin the chemical approach and start drinking.

Gumming your food

For those of you who are in the process of losing your teeth, we know that this can cause considerable worry and anguish. Hey, loosen up. Life without teeth can be much easier if you know these few secrets:

First, when you have lost all of your teeth, you must now eat the right kind of foods. Corn nuts and beef jerky are tough to get down the hatch when you're a gummer. We recommend that you concentrate mostly on your gelatin, liquid, and pre-digested food groups.

Second, get in the habit of letting your rice crispies soak until they quit talking.

Third, if there is something you really want, but can't figure how to masticate it, just have a friend chew your food for you. Many other species of animals do this with great success.

Fourth, eat everything through a straw. If it won't go through a straw, don't even put it into your mouth.

Fifth, Try stirring up your ice cream and toppings until they all goo together and become the consistency of liquid glop. Remember how you enjoyed doing this as a kid? Although they will become disgusted, some to the point of nausea, most of your adult kids won't yell at you for doing this any more. If they do, you have a good medical reason for doing it and you can be perfectly justified in yelling back.

Finally, if eating becomes just too much bother for you, you can stop it altogether. This is easy to do in these modern times thanks to the miracle of the IV. Hooking up to an IV has the added side benefit of being a good attention getter for those suffering from lack of attention and other forms of neglect. With a large, rubber tube coming out of your arm, you'll get more sympathy than you ever thought possible. The only draw back is that it won't last forever. Eventually, you will be expected to either start eating again and appear to show some improvement, or else die.

Composting With Class

Since your eventual and complete physical deterioration is inevitable, don't whine; don't whimper; don't grovel. Get used to it. Plan for it. Enjoy it. Make each milestone of physical deterioration a spiritual experience...for yourself and for others. To get the most out of each point of your ultimate total physical demise, we offer the following suggestions:

When your teeth rot, wear, decay and fall out, paint little eyes on your chin, put a doll-costume over your face and have some fun entertaining your grand kids at reunions by lying on your back upside down and performing to a lip sync.

With no teeth, you can also be useful as a volunteer helping immigrants learn English as a second language. Having you around will build their self esteem since you were born here and no one can understand your toothless English either.

When your colon or prostate rots, you can focus on enjoying the wonderful, childlike, uninhibited feeling of water running down your legs. Or don't wear anything at all and imagine that you have become a living work of art, a portable statue...with water coming out. Strike a position and hold it. Then move periodically throughout the day to parks, downtown and museums. You'll be more popular than most mimes or HareKrishnas.

When your hair falls out, save it. Use it to make sweaters or underwear. The Nazis did it during W.W.II and I understand it was very popular.

Finally, it's pretty silly to have a bladder or brain just sitting there composting in all that goop when they don't even work any more. When one of your formerly useful body parts quits working, have it taken out so it can be of use to someone. Your organs can work nicely as quart-bottle lamps, fish bait, cat food, softball bases, and paper weights, just to name a few of the hundreds of possibilities. ◆

5

Deciding What Kind of Geezer You Want to Be

Even if you are not yet convinced that you are a full-fledged geezer, if it seems to you that time goes faster and faster the older you get, if it takes you 3 or more tries to get the name of your children right, if it has been over 2 years since you were able to sleep through the night without waking up to go to the bathroom, you're at least on the threshold of becoming chronologically disadvantaged...or else you're pregnant, and so it's probably a good time for you to start planning for the eventuality (geezerhood, not pregnancy). In order to make your transition to geezerhood as smooth as possible, we recommend that you decide early on just what type of geezer you want to be...to allow you adequate time to prepare. In the event that you haven't yet given this big decision much thought, we have created this helpful list from which you can get a close look at some of the more common types of geezers. From this list, you can choose which type you want to become.

Type#1. The Ornery Old Coot.

Characterized by Old Mr. Wilson in
"Dennis the Menace."

Many spouses of ornery old coots would have you believe that this orneriness is just on the surface, that their particular old coot is really a nice person deep down inside. Our experience, however, has been that this is generally not the case. Most ornery old coots are really just ornery, crotchety old coots. Often, if anything, they are actually even ornerier on the inside than they seem to be on the outside. The main reason why they display a moderate amount of orneriness instead of being totally out of control is because, being as old as many interesting geographical formations, they lack the energy to act as ornery as they truly feel.

O.O.C.'s often have a passion for keeping people who annoy them out of their lives. They do this for the most part by maintaining a steady avalanche of loud complaints and intimidating threats.

If you love a good argument and get a charge out of having everyone you come into contact with despise you, maybe you should consider becoming an old coot too. The world can always use another one.

(*Fun tip for old coots: plan a surprise birthday party just to make him or her mad.)

Type#2. The Quaalude.

Best characterized by a spaghetti noodle, liver casserole, or some other formerly living, but now inanimate object.

Typical Quaaludes are deaf, their memory is gone, and most people assume that their life is retched and miserable, but it's really not because they maintain such a wonderful perspective. They honestly and sincerely don't give a rip...about anything. A conversation with a Quaalude might go something like this:

You: "Lude, your wife of 62 years just died..."

Lude: "How nice."

You: ...And the results of your physical exam just came back and you have a prostate the size of New Jersey. You'll most likely never have another normal bowel movement. Eventually you will be taken over by your colon until you become nothing but an enlarged prostate gland ...and die."

Lude: "How nice."

(*Fun tip for Quaaludes: Try talking to him or her in Swedish.)

Type#3. The Jolly Roger.

Characterized by Santa Clause and my old

*neighbor, Norv Duroc, who liked to play like he
as Santa Clause at Christmas parties.*

This type of geezer loves a good story, always has a joke, and is generally liked by everybody, but everyone wonders, how, for an old coot, he manages to have so much energy. They worry that he is sustaining his energy level chemically. Fortunately, there is very little public outcry to test geezers for drug use.

Type#4 The Snoozer/Napper.

*Characterized by my cousin, Jerry, who is able to
drive for days without ever once opening his eyes,
and to fall asleep soundly at any time and in any
place, even in mid-conversation. In Mormon
culture, these are usually the guys sitting
on the stand in church.*

The most common theory about the roots of this condition is that the Snoozer/Napper is actually in the beginning stages of death and making a transition into it.

Type#5 The Rip Van Winkel.

*Characterized by all the men and women you
know who have spent decades stuck in an
embarrassing mid-life crisis.*

Rip, while suffering from the same types of memory loss, and geezer terminal "out-of-it-ness" as every other geezer on the planet, for reasons yet unknown to science, refuses to act his age. He still thinks he fits right in with all of the younger folk. He wears an earring, toupee, and clothes that just a few decades ago were on the cutting edge of high fashion. He drives a trendy late-model sports car, instead of a much more age-appropriate '68 Pontiac Bonneville so that when people see him, they usually think something like, "Where is that old guy going in his kid's car?"

Shunning the traditional metallic other-worldly colors, she dies her hair a "living" color and fixes it in younger girl styles, so that along with the short skirts and latest popular fashions she wears, when you see her from behind, you expect to see a young lady. Instead, when she turns around, your immediate reaction is something like, "Why is that old lady dressed up like a little girl?

You might be wondering, "Surely the list of possibilities is longer than this. Aren't there hundreds of types of geezers?" We should take this opportunity to explain that while some might think there should be, there really are not very many options at such a ripe old age. However, from this list of the more common types of geezers, you can have some fun choosing just what kind of a geezer you want to be. Or if you feel ambitious, you could even be the innovative one who develops a new strain. ◆

6

Pick-up Lines for Old Goats

Who says that companionship should end just because you are wearing a diaper. Many people who fall under the Geezer umbrella find social events invigorating. Selma Wedge from Hornebuckle, Nebraska, lives for Bingo night at her institution. Players are wheeled into the cafeteria where the loudspeaker is then turned all the way up. Sometimes they play through a couple of meals in order to finish a game. . . although, during particularly intense periods, apple sauce has been known to be hurled across the room when the caller goes too quickly.

It was in a romantic setting such as this that she met Gleeve Sternum, a Spanish American War Vet with a fully funded pension which was just getting really lucrative. Since then it has been just like a Love Boat episode for them each and every day. . . and twice on Saturday.

So you too can find the love of your dreams, we have collected a short, but effective list of tried and tested pick-up lines* for you to use.

Hey good lookin', wanna fall asleep in the middle of a conversation with a real woman?

Hey honey, I'll bet if we connected the negative on my wheel chair to the positive on your pace-maker we could really make the sparks fly.

Gee, I'll bet your arms must be tired, you've been wheeling around my mind all day.

Hey sugar, I'll bet I can make the orchids on that Moo Moo beg for mercy.

How about a drool in the hay with an old goat?

Hey, ramblin' gamblin' guy, wanna see the inside of my Winnebego?

*Note When using these lines, be sure to speak them loudly, cupping your hands around your mouth if necessary.

Should your line be successful may we suggest one of these activities to get things off on the right shuffle

Take 25 No-Doz and see which one can out last the other dancing the polka.

Walker Polo

Stay up all night and watch the Meals on Wheels van pull up.

Sit on a bench with your date at the mall and count how many of your friends who walk by aren't aware that their fly is open.

High Tec Geezing and the World Wide Web

One of the most terrifying parts of geezerhood, aside from your first gall bladder surgery or death, is trying to operate a computer, VCR, or some other piece of high-tec equipment. If you want to break through this barrier of fear and begin to join the technology revolution began only last century, here are a just few simple tips, which, if followed, can make your experience much more interesting.

First, don't fear the equipment. Computers are like many other animals. If you are afraid, they can sense it. This makes them want to attack and chew you up. Let's say that you are involved in an international commodities arbitrage transaction and need to accurately forecast, using a computer, the price movements of the world kumquat market. If you fail to do this correctly, the communists in China will corner the market -- giving them the financial clout to start a chain reaction that will begin World War III and obliterate all life as we know it... including your computer. To solve this problem on your computer, simply take a deep breath and relax, all the while repeating to yourself the following words: "It's only life on this planet, it's only life on this planet..."

Second, Don't ever read the instructions...Always ask a friend or relative to do it for you. This will make them feel needed and important and will offer you an opportunity to bond with another human being. An added side benefit is that it may allow you to postpone having to deal with computers and high tech equipment until you are too senile to care any more.

If, after these two techniques, you aren't completely comfortable with your computer, just go get one of your grand kids to do your computer stuff for you. You have, after all, managed to get along fine for all of these decades without computers. Where you're going you won't need to use this stuff anyway.

The World Wide Web is another matter altogether. Talk about a potential Pandora's Box for the elderly user! After only one, two hour episode, Phil Phecal from Keyster, Colorado, had managed to book airline tickets to eleven major cities, order a pizza, fall into a virtual s_ x scheme, break into the Social Security database, and sign up for three be-your-wife-for-citizenship exchanges. Not to mention that he learned more than he ever wanted to know about the cross platform performance of 'ftp.' Our advice to you is if you are going to surf the Net, use a fake I.D. -- like Bubbles -- and leave your credit card in your other pajamas.

For more information on geezing the net, log to www.wouldrathergeeze.com ◆

7

Retirement Planning: An Exercise in Fossility and an Economic Oxymoron, Moron

Just like passing a series of mammoth Gaul stones or having your lips run over by a train, planning for your retirement can be fun. Fun, yes of course, but it can also be complicated. And so, to make planning for your retirement easier, we have prepared this information. Thanks to all of this work that we've done, you can expect relief very soon. I figure that about the same time the urinals in the county building start singing "Unchained Melody," your financial worries will begin to go away.

Of course I'm probably joking here, but you should know that there is really no "solution per se" for the problem of how to plan for retirement. As you get older, as we have already discussed, your mind is sliding into senility, and your aging body is turning to compost. Unfortunately your financial condition will experience a parallel deterioration.

Don't panic! This economic slide is perfectly natural and happens for a number of reasons. . . reasons many so called financial experts regularly try to explain. Due to the fact that after all these years of planning I'm still financially disadvantaged (mostly because I have religiously followed my financial experts' advise) I feel I am as qualified as anyone to explain this phenomenon. Here's my shot at it:

First, if you have children, you know that the amount of money that it takes to raise them increases exponentially with their age. To illustrate, a look at Christmas may be instructive.

When your child was two years old, you could buy literally hundreds of presents in a toy store for 20 dollars. For twenty crummy bucks, along with all of the free stuff you got from grandma, you could keep a 2-year-old happily unwrapping blocks and plastic dinosaurs from 4

Two more ways to tell if you are a Geezer

When you surprise a burglar breaking into your house and all you can think to do is whack him with one of your soiled "Depends."

A.M. until 10 P.M., or until they lost interest and left to eat the cat's food.

A few years later, when this same child was eleven years old, it cost many thousands of dollars in order to provide this same avaricious high. You had to buy stereos, video games, and other electronic items. You had to pay for trendy, designer-label clothing, each sock costing enough to supply a two year old with toys for a year.

Finally, after your child moved out on his or her own, when logic told you that your Christmas expense should go down, the old exponential multiplying factor again entered into play. In addition to the thousands of dollars that you now had to spend on tuition, computer systems and damage to cars, you had to also add holiday season airfares and long distance telephone bills.

After all of this, you were compelled to just hope that they never got married. If that happened, all of the above expenses would be multiplied by the number of grandchildren and dependent spouses, infinitely expanding because of this immutable law of exponentially increasing expenses.

When you can both sleep soundly AND irritate the other drivers on the road, all at the same time.

If you really think about it, you will note that this law transcends Christmas and permeates every aspect of life in America. Your children will cost you more and more forever until you either die or become a street person.

However, in spite of this law, there would still be quite a few rich old people in this country if it weren't for some other outside factors. Consider our government. Uncle Sam has done numerous studies on old people and has concluded that they will eventually lose their formerly shrewd faculties. They have also discovered that sooner or later, the only thing old geezers like you will be able to do is sit in wheel chairs and drool. And so they figure that, if that's all you can do, you sure won't be needing all of that extra money. So, Uncle Sam has therefore structured millions and billions of programs designed to help relieve you from the strain of managing your excess money. Because of time considerations and lack of interest, we will consider only two:

First, despite the fact that you now spend considerably more on your children than you do on yourself, Uncle Sam refuses to even acknowledge them for tax purposes, unless you invite your adult children to live with you through eternity. He rationalizes taking away your tax deductions because of all of the money you save on discounted movie tickets.

The second federal program designed to facilitate transfer of assets to the government before you are too senile to do it yourself, is the Social Security System. It works like this: You pay millions of dollars into this fund over the course of your working lifetime. . . and this sum is matched or exceeded all along by your employer. The government then uses this staggering sum of money, literally millions of dollars per capita, studying stomach bacteria in goats, supplying all of the elementary schools with condoms, giving to groups who are wavering in their commitment to vote for the incumbents, and of course helping defray the expenses necessary to keep the current group of elected representatives in office and living the lifestyle to which they have become accustomed. When they run out of time for their government responsibilities, they simply retire with their endless nest egg. But before they leave they raise social security taxes to ensure there will be enough additional money there to take care of the next group of legislators that come along.

This ingenious system guarantees that as long as you are working, social security taxes will increase sufficiently to absorb any money that you don't use to cover exponentially increasing children's expenses and that you will have just enough money left when you are old and senile that you can sit in a government-owned wheel chair and drool...but not much else.

There, doesn't that make your planning easier? ◆

8

Tax Strategies for Senile Old Saps

Most geezers look forward to tax time with the same enthusiasm that they might have for being neutered, or having their nostrils sewn shut, and rightly so.

I have found that possessing a little bit of information can help alleviate these fears -- provided that the information bears no resemblance to what really happens with income taxes. That truth can often be scarier than a second heart attack.

We have found that what many people dread most, (other than spending the entire year worrying because they have no clue if their tax preparer filed a correct return or whether he declared that they squirreled away $25 million in the Bahamas) is bookkeeping. I want to go on record right here stating unequivocally that rap music is annoying...and that proper bookkeeping can be as easy and as safe as going over Niagara Falls in a barrel that has lots of padding. To be a creative tax bookkeeper you just need to spend a few moments each year improving your bookkeeping skills. Then filing a timely and creative tax return will be easy, even for a senile putz like you.

To start with, you only need two tools. You cannot get by without getting yourself some accounting hardware, like a piece of high-tech equipment with which you can organize your important papers and where they will be safe. No, no, forget about a computer. They are way too complicated. We recommend an accounting, data processing, income tax shoe box. It can be a very small accounting shoe box, but you must have one. After all, this contains your information database.

I know what you are saying. I can hear thousands of little voices across the land whining,

More active dates for Geezers

Go to a strange place and spend the day being disoriented together

Go crash the funeral of somebody you don't even know

"So just what do we do with this shoe box?" It's simple. Throughout the year you simply collect every scrap of paper that you come across, throw them into your data base and then quickly put the lid on it so they don't get out. You save this stuff all year so that on April 15, at around 3:30 in the afternoon, you can, with considerable pomp and ceremony, present it to your accountant who, being an accountant, loves stuff like this and will know exactly what to do with it.

At least, that's what I do. The only problem is that sometimes he complains that I left some things out. There are things that should be in this shoe box he can't find. So to take care of these deficiencies, I recommend that you toss in some extra odds 'n' ends to round out your tax file...things like pogs, cigarette butts, used Dr. Scholls corn pads or marbles, whatever you can find lying around.

The second thing that you will need to

> Put your right hand behind your back, place your false teeth in your left hand, and have a competition between you and your date to see who can kill the most flies using only the teeth in your left hand as a weapon.

ensure that you file an interesting return is a big notebook. Again, I know that there are many of you (probably those same souls allowing people to use small-caliber firearms to punch holes in their tender body parts so that they can hang nifty things on them, or who keep having to turn the vacuum cleaner off because the hose keeps sucking in their lips and sticking to the front of their faces) who are terrified by such high-tech equipment as notepads. But again, don't worry. We will explain step by step exactly what you need to do. In fact, there is only one step to explain. We recommend that you write down everything you do every day and every night during the course of the year. Now, this may sound like quite a project, but then, so is passing a large kidney stone or getting your name in the Guinness Book Of World Records for having the World's largest lint ball. Your tax return will be no more accurate than the records you keep. You want them to be complete and, above all, interesting.

You don't need to give this notebook to your accountant; it's yours to keep in case you're audited. If you are ever audited, he will be nowhere to be found. (He will have changed his identity and will be picking mangoes on some nameless south Pacific island.) If you have kept this detailed notebook, you will then be able to prove where you claim to have been every minute during the year under examination. And this is important, because naturally your agent will want to know that you haven't been out dealing drugs, doing body piercing on the black market, or working for the Republican Party. Because of the great importance of this record, it's also a good idea to get your congressperson to sign an affidavit vouching for it's accuracy.

At this point I should make one final note about choosing an accountant: You want to make darned sure that you get a good one. There are two characteristics that a good accountant must always have. He must be bald...and he must be boring. Studies have shown that accountants with hair are too worried about how they look to give proper attention to your taxes. The main reason why they must be boring is because your only chance of surviving an audit, if your accountant remains in the country, is if he can put the tax person to sleep and then sneak your shoe box and notebook by him or her while he or she isn't paying attention. ◆

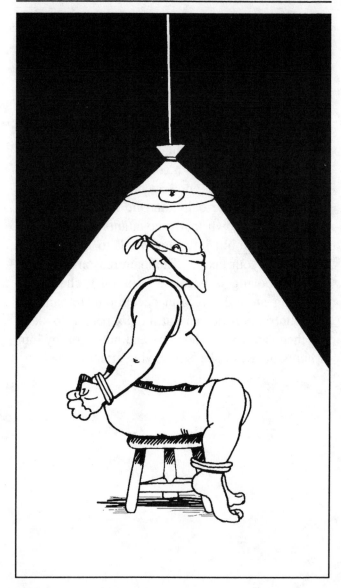

9

Tax Strategies for Senile Old Saps: Part II

Let's assume that the tax man has accused you of being $600.00 short in calculating your income taxes and you receive notice that you have made a $600.00 mistake. Add to that initial figure, penalties for improper filing of $24,000.00, the penalty for late payment of $108,000.00, the penalty for poor color coordination of $803,000.00, the penalty allowed under IRC sec. 007, sub section 9 known as the SAP provision, $4,000,002.00 which is intended to subsidize the Social Security Administration who continually makes accounting over sights, and after you throw in an illegal procedure penalty for 5 yards, your bill has become large enough to get your attention. Even though you are fairly certain that the mistake is theirs and that you don't really owe millions of dollars in additional taxes, now may be a good time to begin to consider your options.

There are two main ways that you can choose to deal with this problem: First, you can do what many paranoid, terrified, shell-shocked tax-payers do and wring your trembling hands while you get out your check book sobbing as you write out the check knowing that if you get into a fight with these guys, especially if you win, they will get mad. And then they could choose to look at your past 25 tax returns, in which case they would find out that in 1969 you wrote off the expenses from your purchase of 6 new snow mobiles as a medical deduction.

Second, you can choose to stand on principle...to set about to prove to the IRS that you are honest and the return that you filed is correct. If you choose this route, you must know that doing

More ways to tell if you are a Geezer

When you abandon all hope of ever boarding another commercial jetliner because your metal teeth, heat conducting Gaul stones, pace-maker, hip replacement, hearing aid, and walker make it impossible to get through security.

the right thing can sometimes be expensive. In this case you should be prepared to sacrifice 15 years of your life and be able to put up a tidy sum of money...around $4,000,000 will usually do it. And of course you will need a good lawyer who has a chance of winning. We recommend Johnny Cochran or F. Lee Bailey.

*If you are a principled, moral American citizen who is convinced that you are right, and you choose this second option, you will inevitably be facing huge, never ending legal and accounting expenses. We therefore feel it our patriotic duty to give you a few money raising suggestions to help build your legal defense fund.

Suggestion#1

Make a video tape telling your side of the story and sell it via a 900 number. This works best if you are also a defendant in a high-profile murder case.

When you don't really want to win the vacation on the game show because going on vacation is too much effort.

When your wrinkles are larger and firmer than your muscles.

Suggestion#2

Try the highly successful billing approach pioneered by the IRS where they buy a mailing list and send random billing notices of varying, arbitrary amounts to the names on the list. You will find that you will have best luck with this strategy if you can get some IRS letterhead to mail the notices out on, or if you use the signature of a law firm. This is necessary to get people's attention. Otherwise, it could wind up in the trash as just another piece of junk mail. (You might even be able to get President Clinton to share some of his legal defense fund with you if you send him one of these notices on imitation legal letterhead announcing that you have film footage of his liaison with those South American beach bunnies last year.)

Suggestion#3

Another fund-raising method has become possible since gambling has become so popular in recent years. Set up a book on all of the little league games in the neighborhood. All of the daddies will invest, especially if they know that the proceeds will go to your legal defense fund. You can even have BINGO games in your garage or promote fights between rival gang members. Most state lottery regulators won't mind that you take a little of their business because, after all, your fund raising is for a worthy cause.

Now, after all of this worry, we want to make you aware that there is a pretty good possibility that these IRS notices you have been receiving could just be an IRS prank. We have heard that these wild and crazy IRS agents get pretty crazy at times. After all, they do have a lot of fun down at the old accounting headquarters, as you can well imagine. If you think that this is probably the case and they are just goofing off, go ahead and ignore the notices. Treat them as just another good government joke. ◆

10 The Geezer's Grail: How to Make People Think You're Younger than You Really Are

As they age, many pathetic geezers feel a compelling urge to try to make alert younger people, who still have good eyesight and hearing combined with all of their mental faculties, think they are younger than they really are. It's a fact that only 62% of the population is over 40. That leaves the large majority, roughly 38%, who desperately need to be impressed. If you are one of the chronologically disadvantaged who sincerely wants to appear younger than you are, we offer the following suggestions to help you keep from making a complete goober of yourself:

#1. If you want to be known as a flashy dresser, you must figure out the teenagers. Look around and see what the kids are wearing and try as hard as you can to look like you fit in. The object is to make yourself disappear into the youthful crowd.

Ladies, a must for you is a collection of mini-skirts so that you can trick all of the 17-year-old boys into asking you out. And then, after you have a mini wardrobe, since you're really as old as dirt and rocks, you might need to do something about some of those physiological features that could give you away. For example, few 17-year-old cheer leader types have legs encrusted with multiple layers of varicose veins. Fortunately for you, we have some suggestions to help you hide them.

More ways to tell if you are a Geezer

As a new dimension to your love life, when you kiss your boyfriend, instead of having your braces get caught on his lip like some teenagers do, you worry that if you get too excited, when you finish, he'll end up with your dentures in his mouth.

The prime piece of real estate that you own is a burial plot.

For starters, you can get a pin and pop them. But be careful not to do this on your nice furniture. Next, cover them up with skin-colored socks. Depending upon the actual shape of your legs, some of you will need to wear very thick socks to smooth out the cottage cheese-shaped peaks and valleys. Don't worry about feeling out of place wearing thick socks. This can be an advantage. You can use them in place of a purse to carry things around. (We should note here that if you live in a very warm climate, thick socks can make your hot-flashes a little bit more pronounced.)

If this pop and sock plan doesn't feel comfortable for you, consider another option; painting over your unsightly legs. We recommend a good all-weather latex house paint so it won't come off too easily in bad weather or in the hot tub. And, be sure to get a color you can live with. While this approach doesn't do anything for flab or cellulite, (These can be explained away by saying that you were in a bad accident) it will fool all of the young people you come into contact with into believing that you are trying to look a whole lot younger than you really are.

Although you ladies can look trendy and fashionable wearing almost anything, for my own peace of mind, I must comment on one type of clothing which may not be appropriate for some. Between large gags as she struggled to keep her lunch down the other day, my daughter commented that Spandex is a privilege, not a right. Most people who can read the big "E" at the top of the eye chart would agree. So, if you are getting up in years and would like to gauge whether or not you can wear Spandex without causing everyone to toss their cookies, follow these guidelines: If you have the following characteristics, feel free: You are Jane Fonda.

You older guys, you should know that Speedo swim suits are a chick magnet. Young babes love them. Whenever I have disguised myself as a drug dealer so I could hang out on the beach and eaves drop on youthful conversations, before I got whisked off to the pokey, I always heard many interesting comments about old fogies in Speedos. We also recommend that you shave your head and of course wear an earring.

How fortunate we are that bald is trendy now days. The younger guys would be green with envy if they knew that some of you can get this bald look without even going to the barber. Your hair already figured out what's trendy and leaped from your head.

Above all, baby boomers take pride in their non-conformity. Just like we did in the 60's, when we showed what non-conformists we were when all 60 million of us grew our hair long and wore bell-bottoms, beads, and tie died T-shirts. Now we can emphasize this same level of non-conformity by all wearing pony tails and earrings to the grave. This will emphasize to those trend-setting 38% who are younger than us how independent-thinking and hip we are.

Finally, a brief word about your automobile is probably in order. Since you are what you drive, buy something sporty. Remember back when you were younger and would see some crotchety old geezer in a real hot sports car. If you are like me, I'll bet your first response was usually, "That car was made for him or her." You never, not for even one moment, thought: "What's that old geezer doing in that hot car." or "What a waste of great wheels to have some nearly dead old booger driving it around at 17 miles per hour."

Geezing Has Some Advantages

Many old boogers often become preoccupied with the challenges and disadvantages of geezerhood, ignoring the multitude of great benefits and advantages. For those of you in this category, we have listed a few of the more obvious perks to help you see the bright side of your slide into senility:

1. You will notice that you have acquired an improved sense of humor:

—For example, you might get a good laugh at your kids as they try to deal with the same problems you had to deal with as their kids do many of the same things their parents did.

—You ladies may discover that you can pull your pants up to your arm pits, put on an old sweater and pass as an old man with a thin beard.

—You may also find that you get a kick out of entertaining the neighborhood kids by taking out your teeth and hanging them on your mustache or the hair growing out one of your moles.

2. You will recognize that you have enhanced ability to out-annoy other annoying people:

—Your television can cause the windows on an unpopular neighbor's house to rattle miles away while you're sleeping in your recliner. . . and you can't hear the phone or doorbell.

—You can cough up bigger gobs of stuff than all but the sickest of younger people. You can snore like a tank. You can fire boogers from your nose with pinpoint accuracy by placing a finger over the other nostril and giving a good snort. And you can make other annoying noises better than the most obnoxious 7-year-old cub scout.

3. Your need to spend money on fashion changes is reduced:

— You find you are perfectly comfortable wearing some of the same clothes you bought 30 years ago.

—Since you don't ever feel well enough to want to go out and do anything -- and since you are so ornery that you have no friends -- you rarely, if ever, need to dress up to impress people.

—Since 1960-something, every time you have splurged on supposedly trendy clothes, you were the only one who appreciated them. Some even pointed and laughed when you wore them with the fly open or with blobs of your dinner on the front. Because of this you have developed an attitude of, "why bother."

4. You have developed the wisdom of the aged.

—You are much too savvy and cautious to get sucked into bad business deals and get rich quick schemes. Besides, they don't make deals that you can afford anymore anyway.

—Your years of experience have made you a terrific judge of character, enabling you to make wise choices on life's important decisions as you second guess everything your children, grand children and neighbors do. ◆

11

Having Fallen Off the Thirty-Something Hill

We have become familiar In our Western society with a number of different rites of passage. Some examples of these are: a child's first day at school, the day that a teenager gets his drivers license, and the moment when a guy first discovers that good looking girls have facial hair and bad breath.

Most of these rites of passage are positive. They signify a giant personal step from a period of lower development and opportunities to one of expanded horizons, additional growth and, of course, the power needed to dump on younger people.

There is, however, one rite of passage that, for most people, has the opposite connotation. This major landmark not only indicates that the days of having one's way with younger people are over, but it also signals the end of just about anything fun, meaningful, or worthwhile in a person's life. I'm speaking, of course, about that abrupt and dreaded first step from youth to geezerhood that is normally marked by the celebration of the 40th birthday. For most people, this is not a happy occasion and there are many highly complex reasons why this is true.

For instance, many 40 year old, up-and-coming geezers become paranoid to the point of psychosis because they think that people are always laughing at them. In spite of how it may appear to your tired mind, which has been severely clouded by age, everyone is not exactly laughing specifically at you or behind your back. Some of them, like your boss and spouse, are trying their hardest to be sensitive and loving and spare you the trauma of knowing what they are really doing. And naturally they are much too busy finding your replacement to waste any time on something as trivial as laughing behind your back. They are simply being practical and dealing with the reality that your declining looks and abilities are driving away customers. Not to mention stamping out what few flickering sparks of romance might still exist.

Don't misunderstand what all of the young people are doing either. They really aren't laughing specifically at you. They are probably just misreading your lack of good taste, hilarious dress, and bumbling attempts to get the point of their jokes, as your efforts to amuse them. They just think you're trying to be funny.

And your own children will soon be forced to spend hour after hour locked in conflict as they negotiate how to divide up the remains of your property. This doesn't sound to me like anything they would be laughing about.

Also at this time, many well-meaning, normally sensitive people tell you things intended to console you, such as: "Don't be so shook up about turning 40. Many people I know are able to actually stay somewhat useful and productive far into their mid fifties," and, "Forty really isn't that old. Why, I know one lady in her fifties, living in a nearby rest home, who still has some of her original teeth!" and, "That huge treasure trove of wisdom you've accumulated over the years from doing all those stupid things is much more useful and valuable than youth, fitness, health, your mental faculties, and good looks."

While these things are for the most part true and while you sincerely appreciate their attempts to cheer you up, those who have had 40 or more birthdays and who still have enough of their mind working that they can reason intelligently know that it takes more, often much more, than simply half-baked and transparent lines of bologna to make any kind of a dent in your depression.

So, in order to give you a few more options in dealing with your depression, (over and above the tried and true methods of Valium, Librium, Quaaludes, alcohol, Heroine, spouse abuse, suicide, terrorism, sado-masochism, dieting and fitness) we offer as an alternative "an actual different perspective." We think that if we can show you convincingly that there are people, real or imagined, who are worse off than you, if we can contrast your rotten, miserable, rapidly declining life with that of a creature like a sewer rat, a mummy, or Woody Allen, and if you can see an entire universe literally wallowing in a decaying misery of eternal damnation, starvation, and rap music all around, you will actually come to appreciate the fact that your hearing is going bad, your memory is leaving you, and you are no longer even the least bit attractive to members of the opposite sex under the age of 80. In other words, we subscribe such theories as: if you want to appear skinny -- be seen with fat people, if you want to feel rich -- hang around your local soup kitchen, and, if you want to look honest or intelligent -- surround yourself with politicians.

If you can truly comprehend and apply the preceding statements, you just might be able to cope with your age crisis at hand, ...and ducks might start hatching from horse biscuits and frogs might give birth to cape buffalo.

It could happen.

In order for you to gain the right perspective about your new-found awareness of your mortality, your sudden loss of physical faculties, and your pending utter uselessness to society at large, we give you...

Things that are worse than being over Forty.

Having your billionaire father-in-law leave half of his estate to the federal government as a contribution to reduce the deficit, and the other half to his pet hamster, Sammy

Not actually making it to age 40

Turning 142

Finding out that the reason why large pieces of your skin are falling off, and clumps of your hair are falling out, and

your children look like Iguana lizards, is because the building next to your house, which for all these years you thought was a

water tank, was, in fact, a cover for a top secret US. military installation that has been leaking various levels of radiation since the 1950s.

While trying to get the last of the egg nog from the bottom of the blender with your tongue, you accidentally bump the "ON" switch.

Having an I.R.S. agent move in next door.

Sleeping in the same bed with 25,000 roaches, ants, and silverfish and realizing that you enjoy it.

Witnessing the end of civilization as we know it, brought about by a nuclear winter.

Driving your motorcycle 70 miles per hour through a paper welcome home sign that your friends are holding in front of a concrete retaining wall...as a practical joke.

Losing a bet on the Super Bowl winner and having to run naked through city hall.

Being sucked out of the latrine of an airliner at 30,000 feet, just as you sit down.

Being so judgement disadvantaged that you actually believe what your politicians are promising you.

Going through puberty a second time.

Having perfectly useful body parts fall off because you have spent too many years standing too close to a leaky microwave oven.

Gaining 275 pounds in 6 weeks

Having your head slammed in the vault door at the bank while getting your jewelry out of the safety deposit box.

Having your dog come to you with a partially de-composed human forearm in his mouth after digging in your back yard.

Getting your hair caught in the track of a Caterpillar tractor, and then not having the driver notice for 40 miles

Developing a potentially terminal illness where the only chance for your survival is adherence to a strict diet of goat mucous, raw slugs, and rutabaga for the next 5 years

Having 15 illegal aliens sneak into the trunk of your car while you're stopped at a stop sign and then, since you are not aware of them, being rude to the border patrol 5 minutes later when they stop you

Finally having your retirement day arrive just at the moment when Western civilization goes bankrupt and all money is worthless

Some things that would probably be worse than turning 50:

Having your son arrested for streaking naked through the local elementary school, and also for being a serial killer

Having your parachute fail to open just above the ground after free-falling for 10,000 feet

Coming into the bathroom just in time to see your 2 year old daughter flush the last of your heirloom jewelry collection, which comprises your entire net-worth, down the toilet

Having the leader of a minority gang walk by and hear the punch-line to your latest caustic ethnic joke

Having The President agree to sell the continental United States to an Arab group, to be used as a resort, in order to pay off the national debt

Having your married daughter, her unemployed husband, their 9 kids, 3 dogs, and 5 cats move into your spare bedroom

Passing a series of over 200 gaul stones in a two week period

Having your lips run over by a train

Being accused in public of being a lawyer

Taking a big slurp of a drink that you thought was lime punch, but which was in fact hydrochloric acid mixed with antifreeze.

Having a pack of dogs get into your house and chew up your 3 Picassos

Being married to Manuel Noriega

Watching helplessly as your armpits explode in a vacuum while space walking

Waking up from a long nap and discovering that your nose is beginning to fill with dirt as you are being buried because you have been mistaken for someone who has died. And that all of your blood has been replaced with embalming fluid

Having the city council approve construction of a combination X-rated movie theater and toxic waste disposal facility on the vacant lot next to your new $300,000 home.

Discovering at 25,000 feet that all of the fuel has leaked out of your helicopter

Volunteering to be a subject in a new experimental psychological procedure, which later, upon further testing, is proven to cause psychosis and acute leprosy in 99% of the patients who undergo it

A few things that might possibly even be worse than being over 60 or 70. . . and maybe 80 or 90.

Having the elephant you're sleeping next to roll over on you in the middle of the night

Discovering that the blood in your stools this afternoon is from cereal that you ate this morning which was made up of 40% broken glass

Discovering that your 2 year old daughter, who has rabies and who has bitten most of the other kids in the neighborhood, has also tested positive for Hepatitis "B"

Being sold into slavery because of your exceptional credit card debt, and being assigned to the galley of a leaky, barbarian pirate ship.

Accidentally cutting an artery in your leg while scuba diving among great-white sharks

Diving into a stream on your "once in a lifetime" vacation in Brazil and noticing, just before you hit the water, bare cattle bones and fish that look just like piranha

Getting arrested for vandalizing parking meters, and as restitution being assigned crowd control at all Grateful Dead concerts for the next 50 years

Having a previously unidentified fault in the earth's crust, which runs through the middle of your house, finally be identified because of the eruption of a 9.3 earthquake whose epicenter is under your septic tank

Having a smoking passenger in your car toss her cigarette out of the window and seeing it blow, sparks and all, into your open gas tank

Going in the hospital for surgery on your ruptured appendix and having them donate your heart, kidneys and lungs to a transplant patient instead

Your Deteriorating Health by Dr. Rupert Barnes

Dr. Barnes is a Graduate of the Cleveland School of Sociopathic Medicine, Excavation Contractor's Licensing, Modern Dance, and is also an amateur HAM radio operator.

Q- Earl Messinger of Clinton, Utah writes us that he is beginning to experience hearing problems, but can't afford those expensive devices to improve it. Do you have any suggestions?

A- There are many things that you can do to enhance your hearing even if you're on a straight dog-food budget, or no budget at all. For example, the first and easiest thing that you can do is turn up the TV real loud. This also has a useful side benefit since it discourages burglars.

If you happen to find yourself talking to a real person, who you obviously can't just reach over and turn up the volume on, you can simply tell him or her that you are hard of hearing and then ask them to yell real loud. Most people are happy to comply.

Another tried and proven method for improving hearing is to use a cone-shaped object such as a funnel, rolled up section of newspaper, or Tuba. Place the small end into your best ear, (not too far though) and point the large end toward the sound you would like to hear. While this won't make much of a difference in what you can hear, especially if you're pretty deaf, it should at least save you having to tell everybody you come in contact with that they will need to yell because you are hard of hearing.

Q- Stanley Billows of Dog Wash, Wyoming writes: Dear Dr. Barnes, I think my gums may be receding. How do I know? What can I do?

A- Stanley, what are you, some kind of hypochondriac? Haven't you got anything better to worry about than your gums? You could have plague, osteoporosis, mad cow disease, or be a Siamese Twin or something. But, since there are probably other worriers out there like you, and since you could be some kind of stalker-psycho, I'll humor you.

First, you need to find out for sure if your gums are in fact receding. The best way to do this is to track them for a while. The cheapest is to make a mold casting of your mouth every so often and watch what's happening in there. You can do this by getting yourself a caulking gun, taking the squirter end and filling your mouth full of goo. When your mouth starts getting so full of wet caulking that you can't keep it closed, you need to have a friend wrap duct tape around your head so the caulking glue doesn't just ooze out of your mouth before it has a chance to dry. (Be sure to leave your nose un-taped in case the goo hardens in your mouth thus hampering your breathing.) And watch that the material doesn't get too hard before you take it out of your mouth. That can be bad. Also, there are some people who don't like the taste of caulking all by it's self. If this is you, you can flavor it with gelatin, Tums, dried prunes, or something.

After performing this procedure every other day for a couple of weeks, you can measure the movement of the bumps in the dried caulking which represent your gums. If it looks to you like your gums are indeed receding, you should now be prepared to deal with it. Bear in mind that all of your teeth will probably fall out eventually any way. For most geezers, this is no big deal, they just figure that now they have one less thing to worry about.

You can always get yourself some dentures if this is a big deal to you. Even if your gums have completely receded so that conventional dentures don't have anything to fasten to, modern scientists and orthodontists have gotten so good that they can hook them to almost anything, your tonsils, adenoids, septum or epiglottis.

There, now go find something decent to worry about.

Q- Melvin Farley of Littleton, Colorado writes: Dear Dr. Barnes, For the last few years, I have been unable to sleep like I used to. I wake up frequently in the night to go to the bathroom and then can never go back to sleep. I'm always tired. What do you recommend?

A- For patients who don't sleep as well as they used to, some have tried the following treatments:

First, for those people who don't mind a few side effects, but also don't want the hassle of actually having to change any destructive behaviors, the best option could be the chemical route. There are two classes of drugs that you can

84

take to help you sleep: The Amphetamine group which includes prednezone, amoxicillan, caffeine, codeine, most kinds of barbiturates, and several recreational drugs, and then you have the Prozac group which includes beer, wine, champagnes, Whisky, and Barry Manilow records. Should you decide to go this route, and at your age, many recommend it, you simply need to decide whether you want to rust out or wear out.

If you feel that you are in the mood wear out, this can be accomplished in just a few days by taking large doses of the amphetamine group of drugs outlined above. Since your question had to do with sleep, I should mention that taking huge piles of these drugs may not actually improve the quality of your sleep. It will nevertheless solve your problem because you will completely lose any interest in sleep. You will be much too busy and wound up to waste time sleeping...or eating...or bathing...or lots of other things that take up large blocks of time. Fatigue will cease to be a factor in your life.

I'm sure that somewhere there is a law requiring us to disclose a few side affects of taking the "wear out" approach, namely, your life expectancy will be calculated in hours and minutes instead of years. (Although people who use this approach claim that they are able to cram as much living into a few hours and minutes as they might otherwise have done in years without treatment.)

Also, your ears will probably ring...and in extreme cases your head might explode.

If instead you choose the "rust out" approach, you will simply need to stock up on as many of these "over the counter" drugs as you can and drink a random assortment each night before going to bed. You will sleep like a baby. Deeply. For a long, long time

I know what you are thinking. "What about when I wake up all those times in the middle of the night to go to the bathroom because of my composting prostate?" Don't worry about it. If you choose to rust out chemically, you will be sleeping so well that you won't even want to wake up for such minor problems...sometimes for two or three days.

These are only two of the many possible solutions that some people have tried to solve their sleeping problem. If you decide to give them a try, I'm sure that many of our readers would be fascinated hearing all about your results. Especially if you are trying the "wear-out" approach, you may feel like you want to take on a project like corresponding with all of our readers to share your experiences with them. You can probably get a list of them by going to all of the book stores that sell our books and watching the people who buy it. Stop them and ask for their address. ◆

"WHEN YOU'RE AS OLD AS DIRT LIKE YOU"
By Wayne Allred (Punctuation by nobody)
(Sung to the tune of "Flight of the Bumble Bee")

When you're as old as dirt, like you
Your hairs becomes so few
Your head is like a cue
But who are you going to sue?
When you're as old as dirt, like you.

When you're as old as dirt like you
Your kids think you're a pooh
With clothes you ain't got a clue
When you're as old as dirt like you

So what if you were a jock, no one
  cares
And there's no dang memory
  between your ears
Once you watched who everyone
  marries
Now you're obsessed with the
  obituaries

Your memory's gone; you live in a
  haze
All you remember are your
  childhood days
All of your muscles have turned to
  soup
You're covered with wrinkles and
  can't even poop

WHEN YOU'RE AS OLD AS DIRT LIKE YOU
YOUR MUSCLES TURN TO MUSH
YOU WHINE CONTINUALLY BECAUSE
YOUR WHEEL CHAIR NEEDS A PUSH

THOUGH YOU MAY NOT THINK THAT
YOU'RE SO OLD
WHEN WEIGHED AGAINST A REDWOOD
AS FAR AS EVERYONE ELSE IS CONCERNED
YOU'RE JUST A PILE OF DEAD WOOD

WHEN YOU'RE AS OLD AS DIRT, LIKE YOU
YOU THINK YOUR LIFE IS THROUGH
FOR THE MOST PART THIS IS TRUE
WHEN YOU'RE AS OLD AS DIRT, LIKE YOU

Willow Tree Book Order Form

Book Title	Quantity	x	Cost / Book	=	Total
_____	_____		$5.95		_____
_____	_____		$5.95		_____
_____	_____		$5.95		_____
_____	_____		$5.95		_____
_____	_____		$5.95		_____
_____	_____		$5.95		_____
_____	_____		$5.95		_____
_____	_____		$5.95		_____

Do not send Cash. Mail check or money order to:

Willow Tree Books   P.O. Box 516 Kamas, Utah   84036
Telephone 435-783-6679
Allow 3 weeks for delivery.

Quantity discounts available. Call us for more information.
9 a.m. - 5 p.m. MST

Sub Total =

Shipping = $2.00

Tax 8.5% =

Total Amount Enclosed =

Shipping Address

Name:

Street:

City: **State:**

Zip Code:

Telephone: